Preparing for War? Moscow Facing an Arc of Crisis

By

Andrew Monaghan

Strategic Studies Institute
And
U.S. Army War College Press

Printed in the United States of America
ISBN: 978-1544703817

The United States Army War College

The United States Army War College educates and develops leaders for service at the strategic level while advancing knowledge in the global application of Landpower.

The purpose of the United States Army War College is to produce graduates who are skilled critical thinkers and complex problem solvers. Concurrently, it is our duty to the U.S. Army to also act as a "think factory" for commanders and civilian leaders at the strategic level worldwide and routinely engage in discourse and debate concerning the role of ground forces in achieving national security objectives.

The Strategic Studies Institute publishes national security and strategic research and analysis to influence policy debate and bridge the gap between military and academia.

The Center for Strategic Leadership contributes to the education of world class senior leaders, develops expert knowledge, and provides solutions to strategic Army issues affecting the national security community.

The Peacekeeping and Stability Operations Institute provides subject matter expertise, technical review, and writing expertise to agencies that develop stability operations concepts and doctrines.

The School of Strategic Landpower develops strategic leaders by providing a strong foundation of wisdom grounded in mastery of the profession of arms, and by serving as a crucible for educating future leaders in the analysis, evaluation, and refinement of professional expertise in war, strategy, operations, national security, resource management, and responsible command.

The U.S. Army Heritage and Education Center acquires, conserves, and exhibits historical materials for use to support the U.S. Army, educate an international audience, and honor Soldiers—past and present.

STRATEGIC STUDIES INSTITUTE

The Strategic Studies Institute (SSI) is part of the U.S. Army War College and is the strategic-level study agent for issues related to national security and military strategy with emphasis on geostrategic analysis.

The mission of SSI is to use independent analysis to conduct strategic studies that develop policy recommendations on:

- Strategy, planning, and policy for joint and combined employment of military forces;

- Regional strategic appraisals;

- The nature of land warfare;

- Matters affecting the Army's future;

- The concepts, philosophy, and theory of strategy; and,

- Other issues of importance to the leadership of the Army.

Studies produced by civilian and military analysts concern topics having strategic implications for the Army, the Department of Defense, and the larger national security community.

In addition to its studies, SSI publishes special reports on topics of special or immediate interest. These include edited proceedings of conferences and topically oriented roundtables, expanded trip reports, and quick-reaction responses to senior Army leaders.

The Institute provides a valuable analytical capability within the Army to address strategic and other issues in support of Army participation in national security policy formulation.

Strategic Studies Institute
and
U.S. Army War College Press

PREPARING FOR WAR? MOSCOW FACING
AN ARC OF CRISIS

Andrew Monaghan

December 2016

*****

Comments pertaining to this report are invited and should be forwarded to: Director, Strategic Studies Institute and U.S. Army War College Press, U.S. Army War College, 47 Ashburn Drive, Carlisle, PA 17013-5010.

*****

This manuscript was funded by the U.S. Army War College External Research Associates Program.

*****

FOREWORD

Russia is once again at the front and center of the security agenda of the United States. With many now seeing Russia as one of the most important threats, if not the number one threat to the United States and its allies, there is much debate about how to counter possible threats, where Russia might strike next, and how to deter Russian aggression. The war in Ukraine and Russia's intervention in Syria, combined with its extensive program of exercising for war, lends policy urgency to this debate.

In this Letort Paper, Dr. Andrew Monaghan, a British academic and long-term scholar of Russia based at Chatham House in London, reflects on the view from Moscow. In so doing, he illustrates the increasingly obvious gulf in how security is perceived in Western capitals and in Moscow. Importantly, he emphasizes that the Russian leadership faces numerous doubts and difficulties—to include doubting that, in Clausewitzian terms, Russia is able to withstand the test of war. This is both the root of the emergency measures that the Russian leadership is implementing across the system, from the economy to the political system and the military, and the root of the major investment program to modernize the military that was under way even before the Ukraine crisis erupted in 2014 and led to a sharp deterioration in Russia's relations with the United States and the West more broadly.

This Letort Paper also serves to complement and even supersede the debate in the West about Russian "hybrid" war by looking at Russian actions through the lens of state mobilization, drawing attention to important features of Russia's evolving conventional warfighting capacity.

This Letort Paper has been completed at a time when Russia's mobilization process is still incomplete. However, it both reminds us to look beyond the urgent headlines of the day, such as the conflicts in Ukraine and Syria, and to look further to the strategic context and Russia's evolution over the next 3 to 5 years. Given the likelihood of continuing, and perhaps even deepening, competition between the United States and its allies and Russia for the foreseeable future, the Strategic Studies Institute recommends this Letort Paper about Russian mobilization to all policymakers who have the task of adapting to the challenges of Euro-Atlantic security in the 21st century.

DOUGLAS C. LOVELACE, JR.
Director
Strategic Studies Institute and
U.S. Army War College Press

ABOUT THE AUTHOR

ANDREW MONAGHAN is a Senior Research Fellow in the Russia and Eurasia Programme at Chatham House, where his work is supported by the Gerda Henkel Foundation. Dr. Monaghan is also a Visiting Fellow at the Changing Character of War Programme at Pembroke College, Oxford.

Additionally, he is the founder and director of the Russia Research Network, an independent organization for the generation of information and expertise on Russian politics, security, and economic issues based in London.

Until late-2012, he led Russian-related research in the Research Division of the North Atlantic Treaty Organization (NATO) Defense College (NDC) in Rome. In this role, he was also the NDC's senior researcher on energy security matters. He has also been an academic visitor at St. Antony's College, Oxford (2013-2015), and a senior research associate at the Advanced Research and Assessment Group (ARAG), part of the Defence Academy of the United Kingdom (2005-2009). He has also served as an expert witness to several parliamentary committees including: the UK's National Security Strategy Committee; the House of Commons Defence and Foreign Affairs Select Committees; and NATO's Parliamentary Assembly.

He is widely published and is the author of: *The New Politics of Russia — Interpreting Change*, published by Manchester University Press in 2016; and *The Elements of Impact. Making Your Point in Public Speaking and Writing*, published by the Conflict Studies Research Centre in 2015.

He received his Ph.D. in Russian foreign policy (Russian perspectives of Russia-European Union security relations) from the Department of War Studies, King's College, where he also obtained an M.A. in war studies, graduating with the Simon O'Dwyer Russell Prize for academic distinction.

SUMMARY

This Letort Paper explores Russian state mobilization. It first frames how Moscow sees the world and then turns to explore the range of measures that the Russian leadership is implementing to address a series of threats, both real and perceived, as well as numerous internal challenges. These are emergency measures, tantamount to putting the country onto a war footing.

It has been plain for some time that the world is seen very differently by policymakers in Washington, D.C. and Moscow. However, the differences are becoming evermore stark as the United States—and many of its allies—and Moscow increasingly draw different conclusions from the same bodies of evidence. This is true whether the topic is Euro-Atlantic security issues, such as NATO enlargement, missile defense, or—most notably—Ukraine, or whether the security questions are further afield, such as the wars in Libya and Syria. The Russian view contains a multiplicity of challenges, from the potential for war to erupt, to instability in the aftermath of U.S.-led wars of regime change. Many in the Russian leadership are particularly concerned about the possibility of such a regime change campaign being conducted against Russia itself. Russian President Vladimir Putin and others in the leadership circle have been explicit that they see events in Libya, Syria, and Ukraine in this light, and that Russia must learn lessons from these developments.

The Russian leadership has a Clausewitzian-style understanding of war, essentially meaning that it is a test of society. Their view is that despite Russia's actions during the war in Ukraine, and its intervention in Syria, Russia is not yet ready for such a test.

This is because the Russian system, although in some respects powerful, is often dysfunctional. The leadership faces numerous problems, not only from Russia's Soviet inheritance including a limited and decrepit infrastructure, but also from post-Soviet problems, including corruption and passive opposition from the bureaucracy. The military has also endured many years of underfunding and neglect. At the same time, there are other important pressures, such as longer-term economic stagnation that has developed into a sharper contraction over the last 2 years. This Letort Paper thus emphasizes the point that not only is Russian strategy not made in a vacuum, but also that the process of forming this strategy is itself a complex and arduous task.

This mobilization has been underway for some time and is best understood as a process of consolidation and preparation. Consolidation is reflected in a series of measures to strengthen the political system, both in terms of ensuring the implementation of orders (including the establishment of para-institutional organizations to conduct oversight of the bureaucracy and the firing of ineffective officials) and also ensuring resilience against potential civil disobedience and threats posed by extremism and terrorism. The Interior Ministry has conducted large exercises to prepare to respond to "Maidan-Style" developments in Russia, to seal the borders, and to deal with civil disobedience.

At the same time, the leadership is also conducting a major effort to modernize the military, including a major investment program, enhancements to command and control, and frequent no-notice exercises to test readiness and responsiveness. A spending program initiated in 2010 envisaged spending 20 trillion rubles—some $640 billion at the time—on modernizing the Russian military and their military-industrial complex over a decade, including not only much improved service conditions, but also replacing Soviet-era equipment and increasing the share of "modern" armaments and technologies to 70 percent by 2020. This includes much of the heavy equipment designed for conventional warfighting.

At the same time, the leadership has sought to improve command and control, and combat readiness. A new National Defense Center was opened in late-2014, a federal level organization that provides a single point of coordination for information and control. In the case of war, the National Defense Center would assume control of the country, coordinating all the ministries and agencies. In addition, the military has conducted hundreds of no-notice exercises from the tactical to strategic levels to test readiness, responsiveness, and coordination between the military, federal, and regional authorities.

There are ongoing problems, and despite the attempts to enhance the responsiveness of the system, orders are still implemented tardily, if at all. Furthermore, procurement is being postponed, and there is a continued resistance to some reforms in the military. Nevertheless, progress has been made toward the transformation of the security sector and the armed forces in particular.

PREPARING FOR WAR? MOSCOW FACING AN ARC OF CRISIS

INTRODUCTION

For many in the West, the war in Ukraine has become one of the defining features of the post-Cold War era. Although Russia's relations with the West had been deteriorating since 2012, including the failure of the U.S.-Russia "reset" in 2013, the outbreak of war in 2014 precipitated a dramatic worsening. Russia, which for much of the post-Cold War era was absent from the Western political radar, made a dramatic return to the forefront of the strategic agenda. Prominent Western officials have suggested that through its actions in the war, Russia had created a "new strategic reality in Europe."[1] Others, such as the former North Atlantic Treaty Organization (NATO) Supreme Allied Commander Europe (SACEUR) Philip Breedlove, have suggested that Russia is "revanchist" and "aggressive," and poses a challenge to the international order that is "global, not regional, and enduring not temporary."[2] *The National Military Strategy of the United States of America: 2015* described Russian military actions as "undermining regional security directly and through proxy forces," and several senior U.S. military officials (including Generals Joseph Dunford and Paul Selva) have suggested that Russia is the greatest threat to the United States.[3]

Russian actions have generated a series of questions in the Euro-Atlantic community about what it is that Russian President Vladimir Putin wants and what he will do next—accompanied by assertions that Putin has established an authoritarian, expansionist

1

state, and even concerns that an aggressive and belligerent Russia could launch an attack on NATO itself. Similarly, there has been much discussion of Russia's resurgence and its "militarization," and the substantial increase in Russian defense investment (and consequent significantly improved military capability) is often highlighted. At NATO's Wales Summit, for instance, senior officials reiterated their concerns about increased Russian defense spending, noting that while NATO member states have decreased their defense investment on average by as much as 20 percent over the last 5 years, Russia has increased it by 50 percent.[4] Russia, therefore, forms an important part of what former NATO Secretary General Anders Fogh Rasmussen called an "arc of crisis" around the alliance,[5] an arc that also includes serious challenges such as Islamic fundamentalist terrorism, particularly in the form of the Islamic State, migration across the Mediterranean, and instability and civil wars in Libya and Syria.

Beyond the obvious disagreements over the nature and causes of the war in Ukraine and the causes of the deterioration in relations between the West and Russia, the picture of international affairs might appear, in some respects, similar in Moscow. Official documents and speeches point to an increasingly unstable, threatening international environment; indeed, it may be said that Russia also faces an "arc of crisis" around it.

However, there are important differences. Russian officials, for instance, have stated their concerns about Western attempts to inspire a "color revolution" in Russia and its neighborhood. Moreover, rather than having confidence in a system that works, it appears that the Russian leadership is implementing emergency measures on the basis that Russia is not ready to face these external and internal challenges—in effect, demonstrating an understanding that war is a test of society, one for which Russia is not ready. Rather than "militarizing" aggressively, therefore, Russian officials appear to be "mobilizing" Russia—a more defensive preparation in the case of war. In different ways, Russian observers and officials alike have referred to these emergency measures in terms of "mobilization"—"mobilizing society," a "mobilization budget," and reshaping and refitting the military.

This Letort Paper examines this sense of "mobilization." It illustrates both the increasingly obvious gulf in how security is perceived in the West and in Russia, and the evolution of Russian state capacity and its ability to create and deliver power at a time of perceived emergency. First, it sketches out this Russian "arc of crisis" and the contours of international instability as they are seen from Moscow. It then turns to reflect on Russian strategy making and the emergency measures being implemented by the Russian leadership. It suggests that the sense of urgency inherent in mobilization is due not only to what is seen to be an increasingly threatening and competitive international environment, but also to the numerous domestic problems and limitations in the Russian system, which means that the system is not yet prepared to cope with the tests that this environment poses. In other words, although Russia has formulated numerous strategies, concepts, doctrines, and plans, the leadership has numerous problems in implementing these plans—which means that Russian strategy, understood as the ability to create power, is limited to certain areas.

THE ARC OF CRISIS AROUND RUSSIA

Given the sharp deterioration in Russia's relations with the West, there is much debate in Russia about the emergence of a "Cold War 2.0" and a new confrontation between Russia and the West. However, at the same time, there is also much discussion of the possibility of wider instability leading to the outbreak of a major war. Members of the conservative Izborsky Club, for instance, posit four scenarios, three of which are depicted as either negative or very negative ("very bloody"), and only one of which is more positive, with a way out of the crisis with "much less blood spilt."[6]

Other observers have also pointed to the dramatic deterioration in the international environment in the last 18 months. Ruslan Pukhov, a prominent analyst specializing in the Russian defense industry, noted that 4 years ago, Russian concerns were about potential Islamic insurgency in the south, or a re-ignition of the Nagorno-Karabakh conflict between Armenia and Azerbaijan, or even a second war with Georgia — while at the same time being cautious about China. Recently, however, added to this list of challenges, there is concern about potential conflict in the Arctic; and, in Ukraine, there is an already open conflict on Russia's Western borders, which has led to hostile relations with NATO. Thus there are threats "all round Russia's borders," and the Chief of General Staff "should be having nightmares," since it is not easy to prepare defenses for such circumstances.[7]

Official documents and statements suggest that such concerns are shared by the leadership, indeed that they reflect longer-term perceptions that predate the war in Ukraine. They have in fact been present throughout the prolonged overhaul of Moscow's strategic planning conducted since the mid-2000s, and feature prominently in the cascade of strategies, concepts, doctrines, and programs that have been published since, as well as major international speeches (such as Putin's well known speech at the Munich Security Conference in February 2007) and initiatives, such as the proposal to debate a new European security treaty.[8] This overhaul reflected two important points. First, it demonstrated the perceived need in Moscow for a more systemic approach to strategic planning, and served to frame and give official sanction to a series of assumptions and views about how Russia saw the world, its priorities, and its concerns.

Second, it illustrated the emergence of the Russian Security Council as the "chief interagency coordinator" of decisions on the main tasks in domestic and foreign policy. Established in 1992, the Russian Security Council can be said to have emerged as an important body under Putin's leadership. This has been particularly clear since 2008 when close ally of Putin and former director of the security service Nikolai Patrushev was appointed as the council's Secretary. The council has since become the formal representation of the Russian leadership, bringing together as it does ministerial resources, experience, and authority stretching across the executive branch and out into the regions. The Security Council has a two-tier structure. Its core consists of the "permanent members," who are largely drawn from the security services, with only Prime Minister Dmitri Medvedev representing the socio-economic agenda. The wider second tier also includes the finance minister and a number of presidential plenipotentiaries and regional governors. The organization has become the central locus for forging and then disseminating consensus, amending where necessary, coordinating, and implementing strategic planning documents (strategies, concepts, doctrines, and programs).[9]

In terms of security and for the focus of this Letort Paper, the *National Security Strategy to 2020* (published in 2009) is the central piece of this strategic overhaul. It depicts an enduring series of concerns that relate to increasing competition over values and energy resources that may lead to the use of military force.[10] This has subsequently been reiterated by senior Russian military figures: Chief of General Staff Valery Gerasimov suggested in 2013, for example, that "Russia may become drawn into military conflicts as world powers begin to vie for energy resources," many of which are in Russia or in Russia's immediate neighborhood. By 2030, he suggested that the "level of existing and potential threats will significantly increase," as "powers . . . struggle for fuel, energy and labor resources, as well as new markets in which to sell their goods." In such a context, "some powers will actively use their military potential," he stated.[11]

The revised *Military Doctrine*, published in December 2014, echoes important aspects of this. It notes that the international environment is characterized by the strengthening of global competition, tensions in interstate and interregional interaction, rivalry in terms of values and models of development, and an evolution in international influence, with the growth of influence of different states. Furthermore, it notes the continuation of unresolved conflicts and the tendency to resolve them by the use of armed force, including on Russia's borders. Thus, although the likelihood of a major war being directly unleashed on Russia becomes less likely, "in a number of areas, the military risks faced by Russia are increasing," and one of the "main military threats" is a dramatic deterioration in military-political conditions and the consequent creation of conditions for using military force.[12]

Putin himself has elaborated on these themes. Speaking in 2014, he stated that "new hotspots" were appearing across the world, and that there is a "deficit of security in Europe, the Middle East, South East Asia, the Asia Pacific region and in Africa," combined with an increasing intensity of conflict and competition—military and economic, political and informational—throughout the world.

> The potential for conflict in the world is growing, old contradictions are growing ever more acute and new ones are being provoked. . . . international law is not working, the most basic norms of decency are not being complied with and the principle of all-permissiveness is gaining the upper hand.[13]

Later that year, he stated that the lessons of history suggest that:

> changes in the world order, and what we're seeing today are events on this scale, have usually been accompanied if not by global war and conflict, then by chains of intensive low level conflicts. . . . [and] today we see a sharp increase in the likelihood of a whole set of violent conflicts with either direct or indirect participation by the world's major powers.[14]

There appears to be a sense, therefore, shared by observers and officials alike, of a combination of immediate international instability that poses a threat to Russia and its interests; and also the looming prospect of possible strikes on Russia in a longer-term international environment increasingly given to competition, conflict, and, perhaps, war. These would be traditional multinational conflicts between states for regional dominance and conflicts of internal instability in states, particularly when they are located at the intersections of geopolitical interest. These latter conflicts of internal instability pose dual problems, both in terms of the fighting itself, and because terrorism and criminality thrive in the consequent loss of law and order, and spread to other areas.[15]

This instability is particularly dangerous because of the wider international context. First, in Moscow's view there are important shifts in global power, and while Western and particularly Anglo-Saxon influence is seen to be in a long-term decline, other power centers in the world are rising and vying for resources — in other words, a multi-polar world is by its nature more competitive. Second, at this time of increased competition, Moscow sees an arms race taking place as the major powers are investing in modernizing their armed forces, including developing precision weapons that have a similar strategic impact as weapons of mass destruction.

Third, this is all taking place at a time when the traditional strategic balance of power no longer works. If the *Military Doctrine* stated that the existing international security system "does not ensure equal security for all," again Putin embellished the picture, stating that there is "no reliable safety net" in place to mitigate these looming threats. "There is no guarantee and no certainty that the current system of global and regional security is able to protect us from upheavals. This system has become seriously weakened, fragmented and deformed," he stated, before noting that the international and regional political, economic, and cultural cooperation organizations are enduring difficult times.[16]

At the same time, there are often-stated and well-known concerns about the destabilizing role of the West, particularly the United States, both in international affairs more broadly and also more directly regarding Russia. Notably, some depict the growing encirclement of Russia, emphasized by NATO enlargement and by U.S. deployments around the world. On one hand, the West is seen in Moscow to be causing an imbalance in Euro-Atlantic security through the expansion of exclusive organizations such as NATO (and the European Union [EU]), a process that both emphasizes divisions in European security while failing to resolve old problems, while also bringing the military infrastructure of NATO member states closer to Russia's borders.[17] On the other hand, the U.S.-led West is seen in Moscow as intervening in the internal affairs of states, exacerbating instability by engendering "color revolutions" in states that resist U.S. hegemony, and financing and supplying weapons to rebel groups and mercenaries.[18]

Thus, the Russian Security Council summed up Moscow's view of the threats that the United States and its allies pose to Russia in its reply to the U.S. *National Military Strategy*. Asserting the attempt by the United States to establish wider global dominance and push for the political and economic isolation of Russia, it noted both the important role of military strength in the protection of U.S. interests and also the ongoing likelihood of the United States continuing to use "color revolutions" against states that oppose it.[19]

Indeed, senior figures in the Russian leadership, including Putin himself, have often pointed to the threat posed by "color revolutions." Again, this is not a new development in the context of the war in Ukraine. In December 2012, Nikolai Patrushev noted his concern about regime change through a color revolution. "Events are in motion in Kyrgyzstan, Tajikistan and Ukraine, we are dealing with it every day. Are they a danger for us? Yes," he suggested.[20] Similarly, the revised *Foreign Policy Concept*, published in 2013 in the context of the so-called "Arab Spring" and civil war in Syria, pointed to the "illegal use" of "soft power" and human rights concepts to put pressure on sovereign states, intervene in their internal affairs, and destabilize them by manipulating public opinion.[21]

Subsequently, Putin himself on several occasions has pointed to the lessons that should be learned from "color revolutions" in the post-Soviet space and stated that all appropriate measures should be implemented to prevent one from taking place in Russia. In March 2015, speaking to a session of the expanded Interior Ministry board, he stated that:

> we see attempts to use so-called color revolution technology, ranging from organizing unlawful public protests to open propaganda of hatred and enmity in social networks. The aim is obvious — to provoke civil conflict and strike a blow at our country's constitutional foundations and even at our sovereignty.[22]

Therefore, the war in Ukraine is seen from Moscow in many ways as just one part of a wider arc of crisis, one that has been evolving for some time — since the late-1990s. But at the same time, it has served to confirm and accelerate concerns about wider negative international trends. While Western observers and officials might suggest that Moscow overlooks its own role in causing international instability, three important points stand out. First, while many in the West are concerned about Russian expansionism and aggression, the view from Moscow appears very different —

and there seems to be a concern about an accelerated threat from the West that looks like Western mobilization. Speaking in 2014, for instance, Putin noted slogans in the West such as "the homeland is in danger," "the free world is under threat," and "democracy is in jeopardy," and so everyone needs to mobilize. "This is what a real mobilization policy looks like," he suggested.[23] The new *Military Doctrine*, also, points to:

> the intensification of the activities of the armed forces of states or groups of states involving partial or full mobilization and shifting the governance and military command bodies of these states to functioning as in wartime conditions.[24]

If Moscow appears to be shaping a mobilization policy, therefore, it appears to be a consequence of its concerns about similar activities being conducted by other states and organizations.

Second, Moscow's concerns about international instability are rational. Tensions and conflicts abound, from the civil war in Libya to the conflict in Yemen, from the uneasy ceasefire in Ukraine to ongoing (and possibly increasing) instability in Afghanistan and Central Asia more broadly, the tensions in the South China Sea, and between North and South Korea. Seen from Moscow, these form both a series of concentric circles around Russia's borders and offer the potential for the risks and threats to be imported into Russia (such as those Russians who have fought in Iraq and Syria returning to Russia). Because Russia is a ubiquitous state that stretches across many regions, it is unlikely to be able to avoid the ramifications of one of these conflicts erupting into a major war, possibly being drawn into it.

Third, the nature and range of possible conflicts has evolved significantly, and Moscow sees the need to meet a variety of potential challenges: from a major war erupting between states, to the outbreak of low-level conflict near Russia, to the possibility of (externally fomented) unrest in one of Russia's neighbors or even within Russia. As Gerasimov has noted, though the modernization of Russia's strategic deterrent and the possession of state-of-the-art weaponry is a priority, warfare is evolving such that combat is moving away from "traditional battlegrounds" such as land and sea "towards aerospace and information," as illustrated by conflicts in North Africa and the Middle East.[25] The use of nonstate international organizations and the role of non-military instruments are also increasing, he suggested, noting the emergence of information wars and secret operations, as illustrated by developments in Syria, Ukraine, the activities of Greenpeace in the Arctic, and the "protest potential of a population." This means, he suggested, that the time for reaction to the transition from political-diplomatic means to the introduction of military force has severely shortened.[26]

The perception of threats merging and evolving is also visible in Moscow's official statements. The *Military Doctrine* points, for instance, to the combination of state military power, irregular military formations, private military companies with "soft power," and the employment of political forces and public associations financed and guided from abroad—the combined threat of state forces and subversive information activities particularly against younger members of the population to undermine historical, spiritual, and patriotic traditions of the defense of the motherland. Again, this has official sanction and is reflected in the military doctrine, with concerns not just about the advance of military forces toward Russia's frontier, but also the establishment of hostile regimes (even by overthrowing legitimate state bodies) along Russia's borders, and activity aimed at destabilizing the socio-political situation in Russia and disrupting the functioning of state bodies.[27]

THE DIFFICULTIES OF RUSSIAN STRATEGY MAKING

If the Russian leadership views the international environment with concern, it also faces numerous problems at home, and the Russian leadership appears to recognize that Russia is not ready to meet these challenges. The military, after many years of very limited investment and incomplete reforms, requires considerable modernization, both in terms of new materiel and reform. One astute Russian observer has suggested that for much of the post-Cold War period, the Russian military was "shaped by military thinking that dated back, at the very latest, to the 1980s. In fact, some of its aspects had changed little since World War II." From 1992 to 2008, Mikhail Barabanov suggested that the Russian army was a "shrinking iteration" of its Soviet predecessor and was increasingly ill-suited to Russia's new military-political objectives. In the autumn of 2008, and in the wake of a poor performance in the Russo-Georgia war of that year, the Russian leadership launched major reforms to remodel the armed forces, and the leadership has sought to significantly increase both defense and security investment. Despite these reforms, some of which have had positive results, Barabanov notes that the Russian armed forces are still "burdened by major structural problems."

The reorganization of the armed forces has failed to implement some of the structural elements required by the plans, the reserve system remains problematic, and the mechanisms of maintaining and mobilizing the military reserve look "vague and haphazard," including how the reformed brigades are supposed to be reinforced during limited conflicts. In other words, while there are some strengths, there are still major weaknesses.[28]

At the same time, there are a number of economic and socio-political problems, which hamper reforms and hinder the implementation of plans. The economy is stagnating as a result of structural problems, the more recent fall in oil prices from mid-2014, and, to an extent, the impact of Western sanctions. This has meant that the coordination of resources in support of the Russian government's "May decrees" signed in May 2012, and other strategic plans, have become increasingly difficult. While the scale of resources required to implement these plans is enormous, the economic stagnation has meant that, even in the context of Russia's large financial reserves, the leadership faces problems. A large gap has opened up between the anticipated annual gross domestic product (GDP) growth of 4-5 percent, on which the plans in the 2012 May decrees were originally based, and the serious decline in that GDP growth that began in 2013 (before the Ukraine crisis and sanctions) before slowing to stagnation in late-2014, and entering recession in 2015. Combined with high levels of capital flight in 2013 and 2014, there has been substantial pressure on the federal budget and the economic self-sustainability of regional budgets. There is also considerable inefficiency in state expenditure and the burden of widespread corruption that Putin has acknowledged is a threat to national development prospects.[29]

Furthermore, the chain of command—the so-called "vertical of power"—does not work effectively, such that the plans and instructions of the leadership are not effectively implemented, and responses even to crises and security threats can be slow and incomplete.[30] In part, this is because the Russian system does not work harmoniously: Putin has noted that ministries and agencies tend to focus on their own problems rather than working to an understanding of the wider strategic effort and do not work well together. Friction and disagreement emerge as the result of blurred lines of responsibility for federal programs, competition for resources, and because of differences in priorities. There are also problems coordinating federal, regional, and local level authorities.

Indeed, the leadership has long faced serious problems in terms of the failings of the system of power, including in security and law enforcement. This has been exemplified on several occasions, such as the terrorist attacks on the Domodedovo Airport in January 2011, the responses to the summer fires in 2010 (one of the results of which was the burning down of a military barracks), and the Kushchovskaya mass murder case in which law enforcement agencies appeared powerless to stop organized crime. Similarly, the leadership faces problems in having its plans and instructions implemented except through the direct and personal intervention of the most senior leaders themselves. Indeed, some Russian politicians and observers have stated that bureaucrats are ignoring the May decrees, using terms such as "systemic sabotage." Some parliamentarians have suggested that the May decrees have not been implemented at all[31] and have thus been proposing instigating legislation to enforce legal responsibility for the failure to implement presidential instructions.

TOWARD MOBILIZATION?

As a result of the combination of this "arc of crisis" and problems in the system of power, there are increasing indications that Russia appears to be implementing emergency measures, effectively preparing to mobilize. For some, this has been a question of the exploitation of a "besieged fortress" or "foreign threat" narrative to mobilize popular opinion to maintain longer-term support for Putin. This is a "patriotic mobilization," essentially, to sustain high levels of popular support for Putin through to the presidential elections scheduled for 2018, though some have suggested that the peak of this has been reached and that it will be difficult to sustain given economic trends, which might lead to the growth of social or even political protest against the leadership.[32]

But there are other important aspects to this mobilization in terms of institutional developments. These include economic and financial measures, as the government has sought to optimize budget efficiency and reduce waste as a means of addressing the shortfall between planning forecasts and declining GDP growth. Thus, the broadsheet newspaper *Vedomosti* reported in September 2014 that the Ministry of Finance had prepared a "mobilization" budget for 2015-2017, to attempt to balance the budget or have a budget deficit no larger than 0.6 percent of GDP under the conditions of declining oil prices and an economic slowdown that is causing budget shortfalls. This includes drawing on reserve funds (spending up to 14 percent of the fund) and exchanging foreign debt for internal debt where possible, raising the required levels of contributions to the Medical Insurance Fund, freezing pension allowances for military veterans, a ban on indexing the salaries of federal employees, and the possibility of invoking the right to use money generated by the prison system.[33] At the same time, there has been a shift to increased prioritization of defense expenditure and investment in the military-industrial complex as an engine for the economy, and a reorientation of planning toward program-based budgets. Similarly, pressure is being brought to bear on budget excesses, as official figures estimated that a failure to comply with budgetary laws cost 300 billion rubles in 2012 alone (apart from the impact of corruption). In late-2013, nearly 30,000 officials were being investigated and sanctioned for such violations.[34]

Concurrently, there are a number of practical measures being conducted by the leadership to strengthen and consolidate the political system and ensure that the May decrees are implemented. Again, *Vedomosti* has suggested that the leadership was increasing pressure on the government and civil service, even demanding a "mobilization" speed of fulfillment of its instructions—that 100 percent of instructions had to be implemented on time. It is noteworthy that since 2012, several ministers have been fired—or have had their resignations quickly accepted—as a result of Putin's unhappiness with their performance in implementing the May decrees. The leadership has sought to improve direct and indirect manual control—the micromanagement of the implementation of tasks. This has been reflected in Putin chairing a regular series of expanded government meetings to monitor implementation. At the same time, the leadership has conducted an ongoing rotation of personnel to strengthen the vertical of power to provide a better alignment of power. In strategically important regions, there is now an alignment of presidential plenipotentiaries, ministers, and regional governors — in effect, a triple vertical of power.

The leadership has also established a number of "para-institutional" bodies such as the All-Russian Popular Front (ONF) to create a direct link between the authorities and society. Created in May 2011 as a civil volunteer organization in support of Vladimir Putin, the ONF appears to have gained strength and its role has considerably evolved; it was relaunched as a movement in June 2013. Its goal is to promote unity, civil solidarity, and Russia's development as a free, strong, and sovereign state. It enjoys the explicit support of Putin, is directed from the Kremlin, and now stretches across the country with senior members occupying important roles — such as Alexander Galushka, who was appointed Minister for the Development of the Russian Far East in September 2013. The practical elements of ONF's remit have considerably broadened. It contributes to the formulation of plans and monitors their implementation, often putting pressure on regional governors, even taking a leading role in petitioning Putin for their removal if they fail to implement instructions. It is also responsible for conducting an anti-corruption campaign with oversight of municipal and state property privatization. The ONF has also played a noteworthy role in the "patriotic mobilization" since 2014, for instance organizing the "We're Together" demonstrations at the time of the annexation of Crimea.

There are also preparatory measures being implemented in the military and security spheres. Expenditure on defense and security has been significantly increased since 2011, and targets set in the May decrees indicate the scale of investment that is necessary. Two of the May decrees are focused on the military—one addressing necessary improvements to military service, the other on implementing plans for developing the armed forces and modernizing the military-industrial complex. The former decree seeks to provide improved conditions for service members, raise the prestige and appeal of service, and create a national reserve "in line with the concept of creating a new system of training and accumulating mobilization resources for the armed forces."[35]

The latter decree announces a major plan to modernize military equipment and conditions, replacing Soviet-era weapons and the defense industry. The spending program envisaged, for instance, increasing the share of modern armaments, military, and special technologies to 70 percent by 2020, with further development to 2025 envisaged. Strategic nuclear forces for deterrence remain the main priority, and the nuclear arsenal is to receive new Topol-M and RS24 Yars missiles, new submarines, and modernized Tu-160 and Tu-195MS bombers.[36] (Though the May decrees emphasized these aims, it is important to note that an increase in arms procurement had begun in earnest in 2010, and in 2011, a state arms program had framed the re-armament of the armed forces by 2020.)

There is an extensive and ambitious "shopping list," including procurement for sea, land, air and space, communications, intelligence and control systems, electronic warfare, unmanned aerial vehicle systems, robotic strike systems, modern transit aviation, precision weapons, and the means to fight them and individual soldier defense systems.[37] The list includes 400 Intercontinental and Submarine Launched Ballistic Missiles (ICBM and SSBM), eight nuclear-powered ballistic missile submarines, 20 multipurpose submarines and 50 major surface vessels, 100 military satellites, 600 fixed-wing aircraft, 1000 helicopters, 2,300 tanks, 2,000 self-propelled artillery systems, 7,000 military vehicles, 56 S-400 air defense battalions, and 10 Iskander-M tactical missiles brigades. Some have noted that these plans are "too optimistic, assuming no delays, technical or design problems or bottlenecks," and are tantamount to a "wish list," and that what is stated as "is being purchased" or "will be delivered" is "not necessarily what will definitely be acquired."[38]

To be sure, Western sanctions, economic stagnation, ongoing high levels of corruption, and limited capacity in the defense industry have combined to cause delays, and there are clearly a range of ongoing problems as suggested by the collapse of the army barracks at a paratrooper training camp (killing 23 soldiers) and the crashes of nine military aircraft (so far) in 2015. Nevertheless, as noted above, Gerasimov has suggested that given the challenges Russia faces, possession of state of the art weaponry is a "vital condition for the country's existence," and despite a slow start, progress is being made in procurement. Russia is also seeking alternatives to Western technological supply, particularly from Asia to compensate for or mitigate the effects of the sanctions. Thus, at the end of 2014, official statements suggested that 30 percent of the armed forces inventory had been modernized — roughly in line with Gerasimov's statement of early 2013.[39]

While defense and security investment is an important element of modernization and preparation to face the arc of crisis, the Russian leadership has also sought to test and improve the system through an extensive series of exercises. Measures are being prepared to ensure the Interior Ministry's readiness to deal with internal threats, including testing through large-scale exercises. In April 2015, there was a strategic level exercise ("Zaslon-2015") of police, Interior Ministry troops, and other paramilitary forces to prepare in case of a deterioration of the situation in the Russian regions and to cope with new threats to Russian internal security. The 8-day exercises were held under the command of Colonel-General Viktor Zolotov, first deputy minister of the interior and head of Interior Ministry troops,[40] in the North-Western, Central, Volga, North Caucasus, Southern, and Crimean Federal Districts, and included joint operations to seal the borders and ensure law and order, territorial defense, counter terrorism, and the protection of strategic sites. A particular focus was to address civil disobedience and an attempted "color revolution." Indeed, Interior Ministry spokesman Vasiliy Panchenkov stated that the exercises were "based on events that took place in the recent past in a neighboring country" and included "all the attributes of those events."[41]

Mobilization measures are also visible in the military. According to Gerasimov, for instance, in January 2014, the Russian General Staff received additional powers for the coordination of federal organs and, "just in case," a range of measures have been developed to "prepare the country for the transition to conditions of war."[42] The Security Council and the Ministry of Defense have turned to think about responding to "color revolutions," including conducting research studying the technologies of their spread, the methods of counteracting them, and framing proposals to offer military training courses in opposing political revolts to university students.

At the same time, a new National Defense Center had been built. Opened in December 2014, the center is a new federal level organization that is a major upgrade of the Central Command of the General Staff and provides a single point of coordination for information and control. It is meant to monitor military assets, including arms procurement and communications, and threats to national security in peacetime. It also has assumed monitoring control of major exercises.[43] In case of war, it would become a communication hub and assume control of the country, which would involve providing reports to the military command and orders for all ministries, agencies, state companies, and other organizations. Lieutenant General Mikhail Mizintsev, who commands the Center, stated that its construction was one of the most important recent military projects. The closest analogy in recent times to describe its functions, he suggested, was the Commander-in-Chief Headquarters during the Second World War, which "centralized all controls of the military machine and the economy of the nation in the interests of the war."[44]

The military itself has also been put through numerous no-notice exercises from the tactical to strategic level to test readiness and responsiveness, and coordination between the military, federal, and regional authorities. Noteworthy have been the Vostok-2013 and Vostok-2014 exercises, the largest exercises for many years, which practiced combat training and long-distance deployments, marches with heavy weapons and regrouping, and the use of long-range precision weapons. The exercises have also sought to emphasize combined and joint operations.[45]

Exercises in the West have also taken place on a strategic scale: shortly before the Zaslon-2015 exercises, major no-notice exercises were launched to test the battle-readiness of the northern fleet and its reinforcement from other military districts. The exercise appears to have been intended to send a message to NATO that Russia is ready for war and can counter the limited deployment of U.S. and other NATO forces to the Baltic States, Poland, Bulgaria, and Romania.[46] Indeed, though the exercises focused on the northern fleet, they also effectively covered most of Russia, drawing in forces from the Central, Southern, Western, and Eastern military districts, and involved the deployment of long-range aircraft and military transport aviation, strategic rocket forces, airborne forces, and marines. They were led by Gerasimov himself and Deputy Minister of Defense General Dmitry Bulgakov, with a special operational staff.[47]

CONCLUSIONS

In a meeting of the expanded Security Council in July 2015, Putin stated that:

> it is clear today that attempts to split and divide our society, play on our problems and seek out our vulnerable spots and weak links have not produced the results hoped for by those who imposed these restrictive measures on our country.

He also noted, however, that:

> recent events show that we cannot hope that some of our geopolitical opponents will change their hostile course any time in the foreseeable future. . . . We must respond accordingly to this situation of course and take additional systemic measures in all key areas.

Thus, he proposed a rapid analysis and, based on this, adjusted the National Security Strategy and other strategic planning documents:

> Our direct responsibility is to ensure reliable protection of Russia's security in all areas and preserve our country's social, political and economic stability. Much here will depend on consolidating the efforts of our state institutions and civil society and concentrating resources in priority areas.[48]

This statement illustrates and draws together many of the themes of this Letort Paper: in Moscow's view, Russia is under pressure from external and internal risks and threats, and the Russian leadership is responding with a review of its strategic documentation and an attempt to consolidate society and concentrate resources. Moscow's military campaign in Syria is in many ways the practical demonstration of Russia's posture. It represents a continuation of the competition, even confrontation, with the West that erupted in Ukraine and Russia's attempts to create a military capacity that is deployable across the world, both to prevent what Moscow sees as undesirable developments, such as a Western-led campaign of regime change in Syria, and to defend Russian interests. Indeed, the Syrian conflict is the first substantial demonstration of both Russia's willingness and ability to conduct expeditionary warfare to another geographical region and of the improvements made in its air force and navy. The reasons for Russia's involvement in Syria include the protection and stabilization of President Bashar al-Assad's regime (from both Islamic fundamentalist terrorism and external attempts to weaken him) and to begin to address the problem of the Islamic State, which has not only stated its hostility to Russia, but has begun to increase its activity further afield, including in Eurasia. Russian observers also point to the attempt to create opportunities in relations with Western powers, not only France, but also the United States.[49] Undoubtedly, there are risks for Moscow in this complex and fluid situation, most recently demonstrated by the shooting down of a Russian Su-24M by Turkey and the resultant dispute. At the same time, the campaign illustrates graphically the situation that Moscow finds itself in: an unstable international environment, in which military force will play an important role.

Two main themes emerge. First, there is an increasingly obvious gulf in how security is perceived in the West and in Russia. Although some threat perceptions are roughly similar, Moscow draws different conclusions from its assessment of the current international environment: what the problems are and what causes them. Developments in Syria are only the most recent example. In some cases, this is the diametric opposite to those of Washington or Brussels, the result of different conclusions having been drawn from developments and different analyses influencing threat perceptions. In others, it is the result of Moscow's geographical position altering priorities.

Furthermore, it is important to note that although many in the West date the "Russian threat" and Russian aggression to 2014 and the war in Ukraine, many of the Russian leadership's concerns have roots that date back a decade or more, and are the consequence of Western adventures in Kosovo, Afghanistan, Iraq, Libya, and Syria. This also throws important light on what has become known in the West as a "new Russian way of war"—often misleadingly called "hybrid war"—as deployed in Ukraine. As seen from Moscow, this is, in effect, the result of what they have learned about the changing nature of war as deployed by the United States and NATO. The difference in views is made stark: first, by the suggestions of the Russian leadership that the West itself is mobilizing; and second, by the idea that while the West anticipates expansive Russian aggression, the opposite is the case in Moscow, which appears to be preparing for a war that the Russian leadership thinks will be foisted upon it.

The second main theme concerns the recognition in Moscow that the Russian system does not effectively work. Although it is true that Moscow can deliver considerable political, economic, and military power, it is also the case that there are important limits to this power, such that the Russian leadership has concerns that the Russian system is not ready to face the test of war—a modern war that will test not only Russian military capability and sustainability, but also sociopolitical stability and cohesion. The Russian leadership thus faces numerous doubts and difficulties as it faces this arc of crisis around it and is well aware of the weaknesses of the Russian system. The economic stagnation so often remarked upon in the West is but one part of this; equally important are the problems of the generation of political power. Although Putin enjoys very high popularity ratings and has few realistic political competitors, he and his leadership team are very aware of the flaws in political structure within the state that impose limits on the ability to implement plans and respond to crises.

It is in this dual environment of an external arc of crisis with concentric circles of instability, risk and threat, and domestic limitations that the leadership has begun to exert pressure on the system. This pressure is tantamount to a form of mobilization: a defensive state of emergency. It is important to note, however, that although it shares some common features, such as prioritizing economic planning, this is a new, 21st-century form of mobilization — it is not based on the mass mobilization of the population, since this is no longer either politically possible or militarily desirable given the nature of conflict. Instead, it focuses on attempts to consolidate the state and society, particularly through the establishment of movements such as the ONF, and to prepare the military to be able to face a range of 21st-century threats, including through a major rearmament program. Some progress has undoubtedly been made, particularly in terms of modernizing the military and rehearsing its combat readiness. Perhaps the most important aspect of this, however, is the attempt to consolidate coordination between ministries and agencies, and the increasing prominence of organizations such as the Security Council, and establishment of others such as the National Defense Center. The further development of the National Defense Center and the publication in due course of the new *National Security Strategy* will shed important light on how the mobilization process is evolving.

Nevertheless, significant domestic problems remain. These, in part, are due to the ongoing heavy burden of Russia's Soviet inheritance — both in terms of physical problems, such as an ageing infrastructure and the difficulties inherent in modernizing it, and also conceptual problems, such as resistance to reform from some parts of the armed forces to shifting away from the structures and methods of the 20th century (though this resistance appears increasingly to be coming from retired servicemen). Furthermore, given the economic situation, the pressure on the budget and competition for resources is high, which has meant that some spending plans, including in military procurement, have had to be postponed and the sustainability of military operations remains open to some question. Therefore, if Russia is better placed to address some of the concerns of the leadership, an array of problems remain.

POLICY RECOMMENDATIONS

The military and security implications of Russian mobilization processes for the United States are numerous and increasingly urgent, given that the tensions between the United States and Russia are likely to remain serious for the foreseeable future, and possibly deteriorate as other disputes (such as that over the U.S. ballistic missile program) compound it over the medium term. The war in Ukraine has ensured that some of the ramifications are obvious and are already under consideration in the U.S. Army, in the U.S. intelligence community, and more broadly across the body politic. Senior U.S. military figures have pointed to the potential threat Russia poses to the United States, its interests, and allies. But as noted above, it becomes increasingly important that this potential threat is understood in more granular terms so that it does not become a self-fulfilling security dilemma; that moves to deter further Russian aggression do not become provocative, resulting in a further escalation of tensions that the United States does not seek or for which the United States is not prepared.

The sensitivity and difficulty of accurately judging this is made clear by the suggestion noted above that the Russian leadership has concerns (publicly stated at the highest levels) about a Western mobilization, and the consequent need to protect the homeland and democracy. It is particularly important to ensure that Russia does not misinterpret signals from the United States and NATO—but to do so, clear and explicit signals will need to be sent to Moscow. Indeed, the United States will need to conduct a nuanced and sophisticated form of deterrence, one that is appropriate to the 21st-century environment. Nevertheless, while in theory this need for sending clear and unambiguous signals to Moscow about U.S. intentions is a basis for deterrence, it has been harder to generate and transmit such signals in practice. While senior figures in defense and the military point to Russia as a serious threat, others, including in the State Department, have disagreed: in July, John Kerry explicitly countered General Dunford's assessment. Instead, according to a State Department official, Russia is a major power with whom the U.S. engages and cooperates on a number of issues despite disagreements.[50] These mixed signals are likely to be confusing for a Russian audience.

Secretary of Defense Ashton Carter has sought to frame an approach to Russia that is "strong and balanced": strong because the United States is making investments in a military capability specifically intended to deter Russian forces and balanced in that he seeks to work with Russia on issues where geostrategic interests "as Putin perceives them" are "compatible." He also suggested that the U.S. is:

> continuing to hold the door open in case Putin or his successors decide to go in the direction where I believe Russia's long-term future lies, a future in which there are economic and political opportunities for the people there.[51]

However, success in such an approach will involve relearning some old skills about deciphering Russian political and military life, broadening and deepening the understanding about how Russia works beyond the focus on Putin and a few senior figures. This will mean reversing 2 decades of neglect of important areas of study such as the Russian military and security establishment and Russian political culture, and reinvesting resources in longer-term capabilities both in the intelligence (and counter-intelligence) community and in relevant parts of U.S. regionally aligned forces. The need for this has been emphasized by General Breedlove who noted, in April 2015, that his pool of experts on Russia had shrunk considerably since the Cold War. Thus, "critical gaps" had emerged in information gathering and analysis, meaning that Russian intentions and capabilities were poorly understood and had caught NATO by surprise.[52]

It also means that developing a more detailed understanding of how Moscow sees the world, of Russian threat perceptions, and of how and why they have evolved, is essential. This necessity was recently emphasized by Evelyn Farkas who stated that the United States needs to do a "better job of really understanding of what Russia and the Kremlin's interests are."[53]

Dr. Farkas, a former Deputy Assistant Secretary of Defense responsible for Russia, is widely described as having resigned in early November 2015 out of frustration with the failure of U.S. policy to adapt to the reality of relations with Russia. Much of the U.S. post-Cold War diplomacy with Russia has been conducted on the assumption that Russia is a potential partner, even on a longer-term trajectory toward joining the West, and that there are many interests in common between the United States and Russia. Yet, on many subjects, even those that appear to be "common," the worldview is so different in Moscow that it may be difficult for Western politicians to believe that such views—

that the United States encircles Russia, for instance — are sincerely held by many in the Russian leadership and security establishment. These perceptions and the disagreements, particularly in Euro-Atlantic security, are real. This is likely to become even more prominent in 2016, and NATO's Warsaw summit is likely to be a testing time as the Alliance announces potential further enlargement and agreements on NATO's missile defense program. Furthermore, this will develop an awareness of how signals will be interpreted in Russia as the United States seeks to enhance deterrence. The provision of economic and political support to states on Russia's border to enhance their deterrence against a potential Russian threat is likely to be interpreted in Russia as threatening, or preparing the ground for a color revolution.

A further necessity is weaving together analysis and policy across disciplines. The Russian military and security establishment will be the main focus for the U.S. military establishment, and it is important to conduct more detailed analysis of the evolution of military theory to correct misinterpretation of "new Russian hybrid war" and to understand the ongoing practical problems, doubts, and difficulties the Russian military leadership faces. This will also allow for a more sophisticated understanding of how the Russian military will evolve in the medium term, facilitating a policy response that can be based on anticipation, not just reaction to Russian moves. At the same time, further examination is required of how the military works in coordination with other elements of Russian power structures, including the interior ministry and other organizations such as the ONF, which are becoming increasingly important as the Russian state attempts to consolidate and develop resilience.

In brief, as the United States begins to respond to Russia in Europe by prepositioning equipment in Eastern Europe and by conducting increased exercises in the region financed by the European Reassurance Initiative, it should be aware of the escalatory possibilities inherent in the Russian view of the international environment. While the United States sees Russia posing a largely local or regional threat to Euro-Atlantic security, Moscow sees and is responding to a different world in which the United States poses an existential threat to the Russian leadership.

ENDNOTES

1. "NATO and Russia: A New Strategic Reality: Remarks by Deputy Secretary General Alexander Vershbow at the conference on 'NATO after the Wales Summit,' Cardiff University," North Atlantic Treaty Organization website, Speeches and Transcripts, September 2, 2014, available from *www.nato.int/cps/en/natohq/opinions_112406.htm?selectedLocale=en*.

2. Cheryl Pellerin, "Breedlove: Russia, Violent Extremism Challenge Europe," *DoD News*, February 25, 2015, available from *www.defense.gov/News/Article/Article/604173*.

3. General Martin E. Dempsey, *The National Military Strategy of the United States of America: 2015*, Washington, DC: U.S. Joint Chiefs of Staff, 2015, p. 2; Paul Mcleary, "More Pentagon Generals Line Up to Proclaim Russia's 'Existential' Threat to U.S.," *Foreign Policy*, July 14, 2015, available from *foreignpolicy.com/2015/07/14/more-pentagon-generals-line-up-to-proclaim-russia-existential-threat-to-u-s/*.

4. "Press Conference by NATO Secretary General Anders Fogh Rasmussen following the second meeting of the North Atlantic Council at the level of Heads of State and Government during the NATO Wales Summit," September 5, 2014, North Atlantic Treaty Organization website, Speeches and Transcripts, available from *www.nato.int/cps/en/natohq/opinions_112891.htm*.

5. Anders Fogh Rasmussen, "America, Europe and the Pacific," Speech by NATO Secretary General Anders Fogh Rasmussen at the Marines' Memorial Club Hotel in San Francisco, July 10, 2014, available from *www.nato.int/cps/en/natohq/opinions_111659.htm*.

6. Mikhail Delyagin, Sergei Glaz'ev, and Andrei Fursov, *Strategiya "bolshovo ryvka" (Strategy of a "Major Breakthrough")*, Moscow: Algoritm, 2013. pp. 6-7; see also Alexander Prokhanov, Sergei Glaz'ev *et al, Kholodnaya voina 2.0. Strategiya Russkoi pobediy (Cold War 2.0. Strategy For Russian Victory)*, Moscow: Knizhni mir, 2015.

7. Matthew Bodner, "Analyst: Russian Industry Faces Challenges Unique to 'Putin's Russia'," *Defense News*, August 9, 2015, available from *www.defensenews.com/story/defense/policy-budget/leaders/interviews/2015/08/09/interview-ruslan-pukhov-cast-russia-defense-industry-analyst/31105299/*.

8. In the West, the proposals are often called the "Medvedev proposals," because they were first noticed by Western observers when Medvedev gave his first major speech abroad as president in June 2008, and subsequently a draft treaty was published and circulated to other nations in the Euro-Atlantic security area in 2009. The substance of the proposals, however, drew on ideas already publicly stated by both Putin and Sergei Ivanov, then the Defense Minister, before Medvedev's presidency began.

9. "Intervyu Secretarya Soveta Bezopasnosti Rossiiskoi Federatsii N.P. Patrusheva" ("Interview with Secretary of the Security Council of the Russian Federation N. P. Patrushev"), *Rossiiskaya Gazeta*, December 27, 2013, available from *www.scrf.gov.ru/news/809.html*.

10. Dmitri Medvedev, *Strategiya natsionalnoi bezopasnosti Rossiiskoi Federatsii do 2020 goda (Strategy of National Security of the Russian Federation to 2020)*, Russian Federation, May 12, 2009, available from *www.scrf.gov.ru/documents/1/99.html*; for a review of the document, see Keir Giles, *Russia's National Security Strategy to 2020*, NATO Defense College Review, June 2009, available from *www.ndc.nato.int/research/research.php?icode=6*.

11. Cited in "Russia May be Drawn into Resource Wars in Future — Army Chief," *Russia Today*, February 14, 2013, available from *www.rt.com/politics/military-conflict-gerasimov-threat-196/*.

12. *Voennaya doktrina Rossiiskoi Federatsii (Military Doctrine of the Russian Federation)*, No. Pr.-2976, December 25, 2015, available from *www.scrf.gov.ru/documents/33.html*.

13. "Soveshaniye poslov i postoyannikh predstavitelei Rossii" ("Conference of Russian Ambassadors and Permanent Representatives"), July 1, 2015, available from *kremlin.ru/events/president/news/46131*.

14. "Zasedaniye Mezhdunarodnovo Diskussionnovo Kluba 'Valdai'" ("Meeting of the International Discussion club 'Valdai'"), October 24, 2014, available from *kremlin.ru/events/president/news/46860*.

15. Terrorism remains a particular concern for the Russian leadership, as both an internal and external risk to Russia through the possibility of terrorist organizations and individuals undermining Russian sovereignty, and the growing threat of global terrorism, and its new manifestations under the conditions of insufficiently effective international cooperation. *Voennaya doktrina Rossiiskoi Federatsii (Military Doctrine of the Russian Federation)*, No. Pr.-2976.

16. "Zasedaniye Mezhdunarodnovo Diskussionnovo Kluba 'Valdai'" ("Meeting of the International Discussion Club 'Valdai'").

17. *Voennaya doktrina Rossiiskoi Federatsii (Military Doctrine of the Russian Federation)*, No. Pr.-2976.

18. "Zasedaniye Mezhdunarodnovo Diskussionnovo Kluba 'Valdai'" ("Meeting of the International Discussion club 'Valdai'").

19. "O strategii natsionalnoi bezopasnosti SSHA" ("About the National Security Strategy of the USA"), Security Council, March 23, 2015, available from *www.scrf.gov.ru/news/865.html*.

20. "Putin's Ally Warns of 'Color Revolutions'," *Sputnik*, December 9, 2012, available from *sputniknews.com/politics/20121209/178026189.html*.

21. For an English language version, see "Concept of the Foreign Policy of the Russian Federation," February 12, 2013, available from *archive.mid.ru//brp_4.nsf/0/76389FEC168189ED44257B 2E0039B16D*. The concept does not explicitly mention either the "Arab Spring" or "color revolutions," but the implication is clear.

22. "Rasshirennoe zasedanie kollegii MVD" ("Meeting of the expanded board of the Ministry of the Interior"), March 4, 2015, available from *kremlin.ru/events/president/news/47776*.

23. "Zasedaniye Mezhdunarodnovo Diskussionnovo Kluba 'Valdai'" ("Meeting of the International Discussion club 'Valdai'").

24. *Voennaya doktrina Rossiiskoi Federatsii (Military Doctrine of the Russian Federation)*, No. Pr.-2976.

25. Cited in "Russia May be Drawn into Resource Wars in Future—Army Chief," *Russia Today*.

26. "Genshtab poluchil dopolnitel'nie polnomochiya, podgotovil plan perekhoda RF na usloviya voennovo vremeni" ("The General Staff has Received Additional Powers, Prepared Plan for the Russian Federation's Transition to Conditions of Wartime"), *Newsru*, January 25, 2014, available from *www.newsru.com/arch/russia/25jan2014/genshtab.html*.

27. *Voennaya doktrina Rossiiskoi Federatsii (Military Doctrine of the Russian Federation)*, No. Pr.-2976.

28. Mikhail Barabanov, "Russian Military Reform up to the Georgian Conflict" and "Changing the Force and Moving Forward After Georgia," in Colby Howard and Ruslan Pukhov, eds., *Brothers Armed: Military Aspects of the Crisis in Ukraine*, Minneapolis, MN: East View Press, 2014. pp. 88-9, 119-121.

29. "Poslanie prezidenta Federalnomy Sobraniyu" ("Presidential address to the Federal Assembly"), December 12, 2012, available from *kremlin.ru/events/president/news/17118*.

30. For an overview, see Andrew Monaghan, *Defibrillating the Vertikal: Putin and Russian Grand Strategy*, Chatham House, London, UK, Research Paper, October 7, 2014, available from *https://www.chathamhouse.org/publication/defibrillating-vertikal-putin-and-russian-grand-strategy*.

31. "Ni odin iz maiskikh ukazov prezidenta ne vypolnen" ("Not One of the President's May Decrees Has Been Fulfilled"), *Nezavisimaya Gazeta*, March 3, 2014. A year later, others who were monitoring the orders were reporting that most of the instructions were only implemented on paper, in effect boxes were ticked rather than producing any practical results. "ONF: 80 protsentov maiskikh ukazov Vladimira Putina vypolneni lish formalno" ("ONF: 80 percent of Vladimir Putin's May Decrees are Fulfilled Only on Paper"), *OTR-Online*, May 13, 2015, available from *www.otr-online.ru/news/onf--protsentov-43921.html*.

32. "Reiting Putina upersya v protestniy elektorat" ("Putin's Rating has Come up Against A Protest Electorate"), *Nezavisimaya Gazeta*, April 1, 2015.

33. "Minfin vnes v pravitel'stvo mobilizatsionniy byudzhet" ("The Ministry of Finance has Brought a Mobilization Budget to the Government"), *Vedomosti*, September 17, 2014.

34. "Zasedaniye gosudarstvennovo soveta" ("Meeting of the State Council"), October 4, 2013, available from *www.kremlin.ru/news/19359*.

35. "O dalneishem sovershenstvovanii voennoi sluzhby v Rossiiskoi Federatsii" ("About the Further Improvement of Military Service in the Russian Federation"), Ukaz No.604, May 7, 2012, available from *gubernator96.ru/article/show/id/108*.

36. "O realizatsii planov (programm) stroitelstvo i razvitiya Vooruzhonnikh Sil Rossiiskoi Federatsii, drugikh voisk, voinskikh formirovanii i organov i modernizatsii oboronno-promyshlennovo komplexa" ("About the Realization of Plans (Programs) of

Construction and Development of the Armed Forces of the Russian Federation, Other Forces, Military Formations and Organs, and the Modernisation of the Defense-Industry Complex"), Ukaz No. 603, May 7, 2012, available from *gubernator96.ru/article/show/ id/108*; cited in "Russia May be Drawn into Resource Wars in Future — Army Chief," *Russia Today*.

37. "O realizatsii planov (programm) stroitelstvo i razvitiya Vooruzhonnikh Sil Rossiiskoi Federatsii, drugikh voisk, voinskikh formirovanii i organov i modernizatsii oboronno-promyshlennovo komplexa" ("About the Realization of Plans (Programs) of Construction and Development of the Armed Forces of the Russian Federation, Other Forces, Military Formations and Organs, and the Modernisation of the Defense-Industry Complex"), Ukaz No. 603.

38. Stephen Gilbert, rapporteur, *Russian Military Modernization*, Draft General Report of the NATO Parliamentary Assembly's Science and Technology Committee, No. 064 STC 15 E, March 24, 2015, pp. 2-3, available from *www.nato-pa.int/Default. asp?SHORTCUT=3706#STC*.

39. Cited in "Russia May be Drawn into Resource Wars in Future — Army Chief," *Russia Today*.

40. Viktor Zolotov was head of Putin's personal security service from 1999 to 2013.

41. Panchenkov cited in Tom Parfitt, "Russian troops practise quelling Ukrainian-style revolution," *The Telegraph*, April 9, 2015.

42. "Genshtab poluchil dopolnitel'nie polnomochiya, podgotovil plan perekhoda RF na usloviya voennovo vremeni" ("The General Staff has Received Additional Powers, Prepared Plan for the Russian Federation's Transition to Conditions of Wartime"), *Newsru*.

43. "Prikaz postupit iz Tsentra" ("The Order will Come from the Center"), *Rossiiskaya Gazeta*, October 27, 2014.

44. "Russia Launches 'Wartime Government' HQ in Major Military upgrade," *Russia Today*, December 1, 2014, available from *www.rt.com/news/210307-russia-national-defence-center/*.

45. "Russian Eastern Military District Getting Ready for Strategic Exercise," *Sputnik News*, April 20, 2014, available from *sputniknews.com/voiceofrussia/news/2014_04_20/Russian-Eastern-Military-District-getting-ready-for-strategic-exercise-3484/*.

46. "Novoe strategicheskoe komandovanie na base severnovo flota podverglos vnezapnoi proverke" ("The New Strategy Command at the Northern Fleet's Base Underwent a Snap Exercise"), *Vedomosti*, March 17, 2015.

47. "Ministr oboroni Rossii general armii Sergei Shoigu provyol zaslushivaniye o khode vnezapnoi proverki boegotovnosti" ("Russian Minister of Defence Army General Sergei Shoigu Conducted a Hearing about the Progress of Snap Exercises for Military Readiness"), March 18, 2015, available from *function.mil.ru/news_page/country/more.htm?id=12010701@egNews*.

48. "Zasedaniye soveta bezopasnosti" ("Meeting of the Security Council"), July 3, 2015, available from *kremlin.ru/events/president/news/49862*.

49. Ruslan Pukhov, "The Russian Military Campaign in Syria: The Balance of Forces and Possible Risks," Valdai Discussion Club website, October 14, 2015, available from *valdaiclub.com/news/the-russian-military-campaign-in-syria-the-balance-of-forces-and-possible-risks/*.

50. David Brunnstrom, "Kerry doesn't view Russia as existential threat: State Department," *Reuters*, July 10, 2015, available from *www.reuters.com/article/2015/07/10/us-usa-defense-dunford-state-id USKCN0PK27120150710#ilCmBY8ZmkwwpumU.97*.

51. "The Scholar as Secretary: A Conversation With Ashton Carter," *Foreign Affairs*, Vol. 94, No. 5, September-October 2015, pp. 75-6.

52. Joe Gould, "Breedlove: Russia Intel Gaps 'Critical'," *Defense News*, April 30, 2015, available from *securityassistance.org/content/breedlove-russia-intel-gaps-critical*.

53. Austin Wright, "Pentagon's top Russia expert pushed tougher policy," Politico, November 4, 2015, available from *www.politico.com/story/2015/11/evelyn-farkas-russia-pentagon-215517*.

U.S. ARMY WAR COLLEGE

Major General William E. Rapp
Commandant

*****

STRATEGIC STUDIES INSTITUTE
and
U.S. ARMY WAR COLLEGE PRESS

Director
Professor Douglas C. Lovelace, Jr.

Director of Research
Dr. Steven K. Metz

Author
Dr. Andrew Monaghan

Editor for Production
Dr. James G. Pierce

Publications Assistant
Ms. Denise J. Kersting

*****

Composition
Mrs. Jennifer E. Nevil